"YOU CAN'T HAVE THE GREEN CARD"

*The Incredible Story of How
I Became a U.S. Citizen*

Gudjon Bergmann

Thanks for everything Cheri

"YOU CAN'T HAVE THE GREEN CARD"

Copyright © 2013 by Gudjon Bergmann

All rights reserved. No part of this book may be reproduced or transmitted in any form or by any means without written permission of the author.

ISBN 978-1493767717

Dedication

This book is dedicated to the memory of
Johanna Boel Sigurdardottir (1921-2008) and
Samuel Emmett Hearn Jr. (1921-1980)

Special Thanks

I am deeply grateful to the people whose names appear on the following pages. Without them, my journey would not have been possible.

Table of Contents

Introduction: "I Could Not *Not* Be Here" 1

Chapter 1: How It All Began 3

Chapter 2: The Phone Call 7

Chapter 3: Reconnecting with Family 21

Chapter 4: Emotional Rollercoasters 31

Chapter 5: Pointing at the Map 51

Chapter 6: Challenging Times 63

Chapter 7: Network of Supportive Friends 73

Chapter 8: Preserving Icelandic Heritage 89

Chapter 9: Deciding to Become a Citizen 99

Chapter 10: The Day I Became a U.S. Citizen ...111

Chapter 11: Appetite for U.S. History 119

Chapter 12: Enjoying the Mystery 125

—Introduction—

"I Could Not *Not* Be Here"

Writing the story of how I became a U.S. citizen has been an illuminating process. It has gotten me to reevaluate my previous ideas about fate, *karma*, and destiny. I always knew that my story was both ordinary and extraordinary—but it wasn't until I started writing it that I realized how extraordinary. Reaching back to World War II, it involves a chain of events that I had little control over. Thusly, I have formed the belief that I could not *not* be here. What little influence I had seems miniscule in comparison to the mysterious ways in which everything came together.

My account details a number of life changing events, including the unexpected discovery that led me and my family from the black beaches of Iceland to the scorching skies of Texas. That part of the story includes some of the seemingly farfetched synchronicities we experienced—but I have also

"You Can't Have the Green Card"

included aspects of my story that pertain to the ordinary, such as the immigration process and our cultural acclimation.

I don't pretend to know *why* all of this happened. All I know is that it makes a good story.

Sincerely,

Gudjon Bergmann
Austin, TX, 2013
www.gbergmann.com

—Chapter 1—

How It All Began

It was in this atmosphere of war, heroism, and controversy that my wife's grandmother, Johanna Boel Sigurdardottir, met and fell in love with Samuel Emmett Hearn Jr. He was a gallant soldier, and she was a natural beauty.

Long before I was born, while World War II was raging in Europe, my native country of Iceland, which is a small island situated between Greenland and Norway in the North Atlantic Ocean, was occupied by allies—first by the British and later by U.S. forces. Iceland had been under Danish rule since the late 1300's, and while Denmark was occupied by the Nazis during the war, the Icelandic parliament decided to declare independence on June 17 in 1944, following a ruling in their favor at the International Court in Haag. Back in those days, Iceland was strategically important

"You Can't Have the Green Card"

and it continued to be so during the Cold War—both because of shipping routes and radar capabilities. After the war, the newly formed Republic of Iceland became a non-combative member of NATO. As part of that multinational agreement, the U.S. Navy continued to operate a base in Keflavik until 2006.

During World War II, Iceland was a poor country with a total population of about 120,000 people. In contrast, the occupying U.S. force consisted of roughly 40,000 men—which meant that U.S. soldiers outnumbered adult Icelandic men—at least during the height of the occupation.

The Americans were understandably drawn to young Icelandic women, who were renowned for their beauty, and the ladies returned the admiration—swooning over good manners and dashing uniforms. But, as you might imagine, romance between the Icelandic maidens and the U.S. soldiers drew harsh criticism and condemnation from other segments of Icelandic society, especially from men, older women, and clergy.

Looking back it is easy to understand why the Icelandic women preferred U.S. soldiers to Icelandic men. The natives were mostly unsophisticated fishermen and farmers, while the soldiers were well dressed, shrouded in an aura of heroism, and loaded with gifts such as cigarettes, chewing gum, and nylon stockings—all rare commodities in Iceland at the time.

It was in this atmosphere of war, heroism, and controversy that my wife's grandmother, Johanna Boel Sigurdardottir, met and fell in love with Samuel Emmett Hearn Jr. He was a gallant soldier, and she was a natural beauty. While relatively few of the love affairs that began during that period had a storybook ending, this one certainly seemed destined to last.

Samuel and Johanna got married in Iceland towards the end of the war in 1945. When the war ended, he was sent back home to the States, and she followed on the first boat from Iceland when the shipping embargo was lifted. The couple settled in Texas, where Samuel originated from, and lived in Port Arthur, Galveston, and Houston, for the next fourteen years.

After a number of disappointing miscarriages that threatened Johanna's health, the couple finally had a daughter in 1953 and named her Jo Ann. Unfortunately, it was clear by the time she was born that Samuel had a drinking problem. Johanna tried her best to make the marriage work, to no

"You Can't Have the Green Card"

avail. In 1959, when Jo Ann was six years old, Johanna's mother Steinunn came to visit for six months. After observing the deteriorating conditions that her daughter and granddaughter were living in, Steinunn convinced Johanna to move back to Iceland and take the child with her. Johanna and Samuel never got divorced, but that was the end of their relationship.

Then, fifty years went by...

—Chapter 2—

The Phone Call

"What?" Johanna exclaimed in utter disbelief. In a matter of seconds a thousand thoughts ran through her mind—but all were erased when she heard the next sentence.

In 2009, my wife Johanna was on the phone with the U.S. Embassy in Iceland. She had made the call to clear up minor details about our green card application, which was about to get a stamp of approval—or, so we thought. The woman on the phone did her best to answer Johanna's questions, but a few minutes into the call everything changed.

"My colleague would like to speak with you," said the woman on the phone.

We later learned that her colleague was a woman named Audur, who had worked in the embassy for years, and knew most everyone in Iceland who was a U.S. citizen—which is pretty

"You Can't Have the Green Card"

impressive, because by that time, the population of Iceland had grown, and was little over 300,000.

Here is what happened during the rest of that fateful phone call.

"Hi Johanna, I was going through your application and I have a few things I need to clear up. Do you mind if I ask you a few questions?"

"Not at all," answered Johanna, not sure where the conversation was headed.

"I see here that your mother, Jo Ann, was born in the USA and is a U.S. citizen."

"That is correct."

"How long did she live in the States?"

"She lived there until she was six years old."

"And, were you born before your parents were married?"

Johanna was puzzled by these questions. Why was this woman asking about her *birth* and her *parent's marriage*? Was there something wrong with our application?

"Yes, I was four months old when they got married," Johanna answered. "My father was a fisherman and was away a lot."

"Well, if that is the case," Audur replied, "then *you can't have the green card ...*"

The Phone Call

Upon hearing that, Johanna's heart skipped a beat. Before I tell you what happened next — let me back up a few years and explain some of what had occurred up until this point.

*   *   *

Prior to meeting my wife, I had been influenced by American culture in more ways than one. Between the ages of eight and ten, I had visited the USA with my parents a couple times and fallen in love with the food, the TV, the movies, and the holiday of Halloween, which I got to celebrate for the first time in my life when I was eight. I have vivid memories of going to Pizza Hut and enjoying a thin crust pizza and a jug of Pepsi, and, getting high stacks of buttermilk pancakes with syrup when we were visiting Bill James, a friend of my father's. I also remember watching hours of TV during my visits, mesmerized by all the different stations I could choose from. In contrast, Iceland only had one government run TV station when I was growing up — a station that only broadcasted at night and didn't show any programming on Thursday nights. On American TV, I was drawn to a variety of cartoons, from superheroes to *Looney*

"You Can't Have the Green Card"

Tunes, and TV shows such as *The Hulk*, *Wonder Woman*, *MASH*, *Kojak*, *Starsky & Hutch*, and more. I even got to watch movies that were definitely not age appropriate, such as *Shogun* and *Invasion of the Body Snatchers*.

My fascination with all things American translated into very good English skills at an early age. It helped that my mother and father tried to keep secrets from me by speaking English (which didn't work for long). My fluency in English reached native levels when I spent a year in Australia as an exchange student at the tender age of sixteen.

Following several difficult years in my late teens, I was introduced to motivational speaking, self-help methods, and Western interpretations of Eastern spirituality. In the years that ensued I travelled to the USA several times for workshops and seminars. I listened to audio programs in English in my car non-stop, and devoured several hundred books between my mid-twenties and late thirties, most of which were written by American authors. Although I never thought that I would live there, it was clear that America had a seductive charm with its unique blend of entertainment, self-developmental methods, motivational techniques, and cutting-edge thought.

The Phone Call

In contrast, my wife Johanna had only travelled to the USA once before we met—but she had been influenced by the States in a different way. Growing up, she had felt strong ties to America because her mother was born there. Something within her told her that she belonged there, not in Iceland, but she thought nothing would ever come of it and hid those feelings deep within. During her only trip to the States—prior to the beginning of our relationship—she remembers sitting on a porch in Phoenix Arizona at night, listening to the sound of crickets for the first time, thinking to herself that this was where she belonged.

Nevertheless, even after we met and started dating in 2000 and later got married in 2001, she never mentioned her underlying emotions. She had stored them safely away. It was only recently that she revealed her emotional undercurrent to me.

This meant that, in the early days of our relationship, I was hardly aware of her family connection to the USA as there was very little talk of her mother's childhood there. The only reason I knew my mother-in-law was from the USA was because of her English name, Jo Ann Hearn—a rare name in Iceland, both the first name and the surname.

"You Can't Have the Green Card"

Having a family name in Iceland is the exception, not the rule. Most people in Iceland are either referred to as the son or daughter of their father. For example, a woman with a father named John is *Johnsdaughter*, or in Icelandic *Jonsdottir*. A man with a father named John is *Johnsson*, or *Jonsson* in Icelandic. This may explain the Icelandic inclination to refer to foreigners by their first names instead of their last names. Very rarely will you hear an Icelandic person say Mr. or Mrs. Surname — unless they are in the hospitality industry. It's always John or Mary — rarely Mr. Smith or Mrs. Banks. Even in this book, you will notice that I usually refer to people by their first names. It's a habit that is hard to break. Even though I am one of the few in Iceland who was born into a family with a surname, I have rarely used it to introduce myself — and to be completely honest I am still taken aback when someone calls me Mr. Bergmann.

During the first years of our marriage, my wife's grandmother, her namesake Johanna, was still alive and lived with my mother-in-law Jo Ann, but she hardly ever mentioned her 14 years in the States. After moving back to Iceland in 1959, Johanna senior had never remarried. Instead, she

The Phone Call

devoted her life to caring for physically and mentally disabled children—a life's work that earned her the Falcon Medal of Honor in 1993, the highest honor awarded by the President of Iceland. The award ceremony was made even more remarkable because the medal was presented to her by Vigdis Finnbogadottir; the first democratically elected female President in the world.

By the time our son Daniel was born in 2002, nothing in our plans included any mention of moving to the USA. I was actively building a yoga studio and a career in speaking and writing, while Johanna was working in advertising and also teaching yoga.

Our plans began shifting when my wife returned to University in 2005 to earn her BSc degree in Business. Her appetite for higher education prompted a casual discussion between us about the possibility of going to the USA—if not to live and work, then at least to study.

A year later we decided that it was time to take those casual discussions to the next level. My wife went with her mother Jo Ann to the U.S. Embassy in Iceland to see if she could apply for permanent residency, better known as the green card. Once there, Johanna and Jo Ann were informed that if

"You Can't Have the Green Card"

Johanna had applied before the age of eighteen, she could have become a U.S. citizen with no questions asked, but that now, she was *too late*. Furthermore, she was told, that even though getting the green card was a possibility, the process of applying could take somewhere between five to seven years, and even then, there was no guarantee that she would be accepted.

When I heard about how long the application process could possibly take, and that it was indeed a long shot, I decided to increase our chances and enrolled us in the official green card lottery online—where I paid for 10 years of participation in advance.

To be honest, we neither expected to hear back from the embassy nor the green card lottery. Our lives continued without much talk of the USA.

Then, in early 2008, I was at a family gathering with my four brothers (three of which are my half-brothers) and their families. My father, who passed away in 2004, had five sons with three women, and two of his relationships overlapped. Despite some friction between half-brothers while we were growing up, we had mostly resolved our differences by that time—largely thanks to my father's efforts before he died—and got together for a

The Phone Call

family brunch on a bi-monthly basis. During that particular brunch, I got an unexpected phone call from an unknown number outside of Iceland.

"Mr. Bergmann?"

"Yes, this is he."

"I am calling from the official green card lottery in the United States."

The caller had a distinct accent, probably Indian, which made him hard to understand.

"What?"

"Yes sir. I am calling to inform you that you have won the green card lottery. The immigration office in Kentucky will be sending paperwork your way soon."

"Wait a minute. What does that mean?"

"It means that you can get the green card for you and your family."

For a moment I was confused. I thought that I was on the wrong side of a prank call or was the victim of a scam, but after speaking with the gentleman for a few minutes I began to believe that what he was saying was true. However, I was so disoriented, that when he offered to sell me English lessons on CD's, I inadvertently said yes, thinking that buying the program was a necessary part of the process. It turns out that I wasted $150.

"You Can't Have the Green Card"

It was the first time I ran into the intersection of private contractors working for the government. In Iceland, when the government calls, you don't have to worry about being sold to.

After I hung up, it took some time for the news to sink in. Because we had essentially pushed the idea of living in the USA aside — after Johanna and Jo Ann had made their disappointing trip to the U.S. Embassy in 2006 — the phone call was a real surprise. When I had regained my composure, I immediately informed Johanna and everyone else at the gathering about what had happened. While we didn't jump up and down exclaiming "we won, we won", we were quite happy. Later, Johanna and I discussed how both of us had secretly been wishing for this outcome.

When the paperwork from the processing center in Kentucky arrived in the spring of 2008, Johanna was named as the primary applicant, although the lottery application had been in my name. This turned out to be important in the end, because it put Johanna on the phone with the U.S. Embassy in Iceland in 2009 instead of me, but at the time we didn't think much of it. Johanna was pregnant with our second child and we decided to wait until our daughter was born before we filled

The Phone Call

out the applications. We wanted our newborn to be included in the process from the beginning.

Looking back, it must be said that "winning" the green card is a misnomer. We had simply won the right to formally apply and have our application processed. We still had to pay for all the processing.

There were stacks of complicated paperwork to fill out. Instead of hiring a lawyer, Johanna decided to complete the paperwork on her own, using only the guidance she found on the web and instructions that came with the applications. More than once during that process I heard her say in frustration: "If I can earn a university degree, then *I can do this.*" And she did.

In late 2008, our green card applications gained even more importance when we made plans to live temporarily in San Marcos during the fall of 2009 as part of my wife's studies. Because we believed that we were getting the green card, we had neither applied for a student visa nor temporary residency for any of us.

Those were some of the *most significant things* that had happened by the time my wife was on the phone with the U.S. Embassy in 2009. We were sure that the application process was mostly done.

"You Can't Have the Green Card"

In her mind, Johanna was just finishing up formalities. When she heard the words "*You can't have the green card*" her heart skipped a beat.

Here is what happened next.

*   *   *

"*What?*" Johanna exclaimed in utter disbelief. In a matter of seconds a thousand thoughts ran through her mind — but all were erased when she heard the next sentence.

"No, you can't have the green card. I am going to send you another set of papers. A passport application — you are a U.S. citizen."

When my wife tells this story, she says that her first reaction was to get mad. She couldn't believe that she had to fill out more paperwork. Instinctively, she also thought that this would delay our trip to San Marcos. She didn't fully recognize the significance of the news while she was on the phone, but after she hung up and started talking about what had happened it finally dawned on her. She was a U.S. citizen. She had lived in Iceland from birth, a total of 36 years, *without knowing* that she had the right to live, work and vote in the USA.

The Phone Call

You may be asking yourself *why* she had been a U.S. citizen from birth without knowing it. Here is why. The regulations when she was born stated that if an unmarried U.S. citizen (my mother-in-law Jo Ann) had a child (my wife Johanna) outside of the USA, in a country that did not automatically give citizenship just for being born there (Iceland), then that child automatically became a U.S. citizen. We owe a great deal of gratitude to Audur, the woman at the U.S. Embassy in Iceland, who uncovered the fact that Johanna had been a U.S. citizen from birth.

The phone call I describe took place in early spring of 2009, and the next few days were hectic. First, my mother-in-law had to fill out birth abroad papers (even if it was 36 years after Johanna's birth) and deliver them to the U.S. Embassy. Then, my wife had to fill out new paperwork—first, to apply for her passport, and then to re-apply for green cards for me and the kids.

Fortunately, the paperwork had been fully processed when we entered the USA in August 2009—my wife a U.S. citizen, I a permanent resident, and upon crossing the border, both our children automatically became U.S. citizens as well.

"You Can't Have the Green Card"

And now, in 2013, I am sitting at a Panera coffee house in Austin writing these words, a U.S. citizen as well. Thinking about *how* I got here, just boggles the mind.

—Chapter 3—

Reconnecting with Family

Our plan to contact her family in the USA was accelerated considerably in May 2009 when we met Jessica Kaye, an entertainment attorney from Los Angeles. How she entered our lives is yet another incredible story that follows a chain of events which date back to 2006, when I wrote my first book in English…

After we knew we had won the green card lottery in 2008, which was the year that my wife's grandmother and namesake passed away, I began asking if there was any way to contact the Hearn family in the USA. Neither my mother-in-law nor my wife knew much.

They knew that Samuel Emmett Hearn Jr., their father and grandfather respectively, had passed away in 1980, even though the family in Iceland didn't learn about it until 1981, when a friend of the Hearn family travelled to Iceland and brought

"You Can't Have the Green Card"

them the news. The messenger was a dentist who knew Carrie, the then former wife of Samuel's younger brother Charles. His reason for going to Iceland was to serve out his term as a reservist on the U.S. naval base in Keflavik. Carrie asked him to try and find Johanna senior and Jo Ann, to bring them the news of Samuel's passing. The messenger placed a small ad in one of the local Icelandic newspapers to see if he could locate both mother and daughter. My wife Johanna, who was only eight years old at the time, still remembers how the phone *rang off the hook* in her childhood home during that period. Everyone who even remotely knew Jo Ann and had read the ad was calling to let her know that some stranger from the USA was looking for her.

Learning about Samuels passing was difficult for both Johanna senior and Jo Ann. Because of the nature of those communications, my wife recalls that her home was shrouded in a veil of grief for several weeks after all the phone calls.

The news triggered a brief period of communication between the families in Iceland and the USA, which included some sharing of photos and letters, but it did not last. The silence resumed.

Reconnecting with Family

Because of this lack of communication, we had very little to go on when we wanted to initiate contact with the U.S. family in 2008. We knew that Samuel had been the oldest of five children and that his youngest brother Charles was a judge who lived in Houston. That was all. The rest had been lost when Johanna senior died on my wife's birthday, January 31, 2008.

We told ourselves that we would find more information once we were in Texas in the fall of 2009. As mentioned earlier, we were going to Texas because of my wife's studies. She had finished her BSc degree in business at Reykjavik University in the spring of 2008 and was now pursuing a master's degree in international business. As part of that two year process, she had to study abroad for one semester. One of the schools in the exchange program was Texas State University in San Marcos, a beautiful college town between Austin and San Antonio. While the school had an excellent business department, Johanna partially chose the San Marcos location based on the idea that we could search for her family once we were there.

Our plan to contact her family in the USA was accelerated considerably in May 2009 when we met Jessica Kaye, an entertainment attorney from Los

"You Can't Have the Green Card"

Angeles. How she entered our lives is yet another incredible story that follows a chain of events which date back to 2006, when I wrote my first book in English titled *The Seven Human Needs*. Back then, I had big ideas about becoming a well-known author in the English speaking world, especially in America, but I had no idea how difficult it would be to get noticed in a country of 300 million. I made a considerable effort, but fell short of breaking through. For marketing purposes, I recorded an audio version of the book in 2007 and decided to publish it through Audible.com. The only way to do that was with the help of an agent. That is why I contacted Jessica Kaye through her company named Big Happy Family. She took me on as a client, but all our communications went through email at the time.

Then, in early 2009, Jessica, whom I had never met or spoken to at that point, contacted me and told me that she and her daughter, Clare, were coming to Iceland for a few days in the spring. She asked me if I had any suggestions about what to do while in Iceland. Without an agenda, I decided to be a gracious host. Instead of giving her suggestions, I offered to drive them around for a couple of days and show them Iceland. Fortunately she said yes to my offer.

I picked them up at 8 AM on a Saturday morning in late May 2009 and drove them around the southwest corner of Iceland for two action packed days of sightseeing. We hiked to the top of a volcanic crater called Eldborg, visited the world famous glacier Snaefellsjokull, which Jules Verne used as the entryway to the center of the Earth in one of his novels, stayed at my mother's Hotel Hellnar at the base of that same glacier, visited the world famous Geysir hot spring area, stood in awe of Gullfoss, one of the largest waterfalls in Iceland and bathed in the Blue Lagoon. We even saw a seal up close when we took a stroll on one of Iceland's iconic black sand beaches. The twenty hours of daylight, which we enjoy in Iceland during the summer months, extended our sightseeing hours considerably.

Near the end of our time together, I invited Jessica and Clare to our home and Johanna made dinner for us—a traditional Icelandic leg of lamb with sugar-browned potatoes, green peas, pickled red cabbage, and brown gravy. Both of them were overjoyed. The weather had been wonderful the whole time, which is quite frankly like winning the

"You Can't Have the Green Card"

lottery in Iceland, and they had seen a tremendous amount of the country in only two days. Plus, we hit it off and had a great time together.

At dinner, we started talking about my wife's newly discovered U.S. citizenship and discussed the possibility of finding her family in the USA. When Johanna revealed that she believed her uncle Charles was still a judge in Houston, Jessica told us that she belonged to a national network of lawyers, and furthermore said that she could post a request on our behalf to see if anyone knew Charles. We thanked her and said we would send her the information, but we didn't follow up immediately due to our busy schedules.

Thankfully, Jessica contacted Johanna three weeks later and asked her for her uncle's information. She told Johanna that her experience in Iceland had been amazing and that she really wanted to reciprocate and do something for us. Johanna sent her the information, and *the following day* we got what we had been waiting for. Several people had read Jessica's request on the network and sent her the obituary for Judge Charles J. Hearn. He had passed away in 2003.

Our initial reaction was one of sadness. Finding out that her uncle had died and with him the connection to Samuel was heartbreaking, but as we read the obituary in more detail we found the names of Charles's two daughters, Charlotte and Cindy, who had both married and therefore changed their surnames. Without the obituary, it would have been nearly impossible for us to find them.

At the time when we received the email with the obituary from Jessica, both Johanna and her younger sister Thury were at our house. They were so excited that they immediately got out their laptops and, at the behest of the younger sister, they started looking for their cousins on Facebook. Fortunately both Cindy and Charlotte had accounts on the site. Without wasting any time Johanna immediately sent both sisters the following message:

My name is Johanna Boel Bergmann Hearn and I live in Iceland. My mother's name is Jo Ann Hearn and my grandmothers' name was Johanna Boel Sigurdardottir Hearn. If my information is right, then my grandfather was your father's brother. Through connections of my husband, an American friend that is also a lawyer, we just found out that your father Charles J. Hearn passed away in 2003. Additional information that the lawyer provided us gave

"You Can't Have the Green Card"

us your names and Facebook did the rest. My mother will also be in contact with you and your sister. One of the reasons we are looking for the connection now is that this fall I will be a student at Texas State University at San Marcos, so I will be in Texas from August until December 2009.

*Best regards,
Johanna Boel Bergmann Hearn*

Within *ten minutes* of sending that message on Facebook, Johanna got a reply from Cindy.

Yes Johanna,
You have indeed reached the right person! Your grandfather was my father's (Judge Hearn) brother and we were in touch with him up until his death in the early 80s, I believe. The last time we had contact with your family was when a colleague of my mom's (Carrie Hearn Olson) was in Iceland and tracked down your grandmother and she then sent pictures. We'd love to meet you and indeed be in touch. We also have family in the Port Arthur area of Texas. You should have found my sister on Facebook ... Charlotte Hearn Reid and I will send her a copy of my email. Why will you be at TX State in the fall? San Marcos is a wonderful area. Look for-

ward to staying in touch, hearing from your mom and meeting you!

> *Regards,*
> *Cindy Hearn Rackley*

With that correspondence, on June 28, 2009, Johanna and Cindy had broken the silence. The family was now destined to reconnect.

*   *   *

I must point out, that in addition to the incredible way in which Jessica entered our lives, it teeters on the brink of absurdity that the woman who connected us with Johanna's family owns a company named *Big Happy Family*—I'm telling you, I couldn't make this stuff up.

—Chapter 4—

Emotional Rollercoasters

The feeling of not knowing where my son was located – fearing the worst – having heard all the crazy stories about child abductions in the USA – was almost more than I could bear.

When we arrived in the USA on August 8th, 2009, we had yet to meet anyone from the Hearn family. Now, in addition to living and studying in San Marcos, we were also destined to reunite with family members that no one had seen in fifty years, and no one had really spoken about during my wife's upbringing. When I look back at those months, they seem like a row of emotional rollercoasters for the whole family in more ways than one.

At Keflavik airport, prior to our departure in August, we were giddy and excited. At the time, our daughter Hanna was one year old and our son

"You Can't Have the Green Card"

Daniel was six years old. I don't know which one of us showed the most excitement. It was the first time that the four of us had left Iceland for longer than two weeks together. After checking in, I remember sitting in a booth at a restaurant, the kids bouncing in their seats, all of us laughing and chatting away.

Our plan was to go to Ocean City in New Jersey and stay there for a week with our friend Yogi Shanti Desai, who had been my mentor since 1997 and had agreed to sponsor me on my green card application. That was yet another *caveat* of the immigration process. A sponsor is a person who vows to financially support the applicant should he fall on hard times, thusly freeing the U.S. social support system from that obligation. My wife couldn't sponsor me because she had never had any income in the USA. I am forever grateful to Yogi Shanti, both for conveying his lifetime of wisdom to me and for agreeing to sponsor my green card application. Without that additional support, I might not be here.

When we landed at JFK, our anticipation was palpable. We used the *citizen's line* at passport control for the first time—something we had dreamed about on previous visits to the USA, mainly because that line was always shorter. That reasoning may seem silly and inconsequential, but at the time, it was a thrilling experience. My wife used her U.S. passport for the first time. My children were processed and legally declared U.S. citizens before we left the airport. I was fingerprinted, and my documentation was validated. At that point, I became a legal permanent resident.

The excitement continued with an episode that we all remember vividly until this day. After we rented a car and programmed the GPS, we were on our way from New York to New Jersey in bumper to bumper traffic. As we were entering a monstrous bridge onto Staten Island, my son said that he *needed to go to the bathroom*. We had no way of helping our poor boy at that point. There were no exits prior to the bridge, and even after we crossed it, we saw no gas stations or fast food restaurants. We didn't even have a container in the car that we could use for such an emergency.

When my son had held it in for over 40 minutes, he was close to crying. We finally found an exit to get us off the highway — but that only led us into a neighborhood where we didn't see any public restrooms. We were getting desperate. In Iceland, we would have pulled over and had him

"You Can't Have the Green Card"

do his business on the grass at the edge of the road—as he was only six years old and just needed to pee—but we didn't dare to do the same in New York, because we were unfamiliar with the local laws.

We frantically searched the neighborhood and finally saw a rundown strip mall in the distance. We drove there as fast as we could and reached a little pizza place just in time for my son to get relief. Since we were already there, we decided to eat, although the surroundings were less than desirable. Thankfully, the food was fantastic. Until this day, we still talk about the pizza we ate at Pazza Pizza, as the best pizza we have ever eaten. It doesn't take more than saying "Pazza Pizza" to bring a smile to our faces.

During our drive through the Garden State towards Ocean City, we marveled at the trees on both sides of the road. We were reminded of a trip we had taken in 2004, when our son was only one and a half years old. Back then we had driven the same route and our son had exclaimed the word "trees" in every other sentence from the back of the minivan. In contrast, Iceland hardly has any trees to speak of—the landscape is mostly defined by shrubs, moss, grass, lava formations, mountains, and black sand deserts in the island's interior. The first men to set foot on the moon were sent to Iceland for *acclimation* — that's how unlike to anything else the Icelandic landscape is. They even have a saying in Iceland: "If you ever get lost in an Icelandic forest, all you have to do is stand up."

After a delightful stay with our friend Yogi Shanti Desai and his family in Ocean City — which included yoga lessons, body surfing on the beach, several visits to the neighboring amusement parks, wonderful Indian food, and long strolls on the fifties style boardwalk — we travelled to Baltimore to make first contact with Charlotte, the younger of two Hearn sisters, who we had previously only chatted with online.

Charlotte lived in Virginia, and we had chosen Baltimore as a meeting place because it was approximately half way between where she lived and where we were staying. Johanna went through a range of emotions on our way to Baltimore, both anticipation and trepidation, but when we finally met Charlotte at a Hard Rock Cafe near the harbor area in Baltimore, it was as though we had known her for years. This dark haired lady, who sported glasses and casual clothes, bore the family resemblance. We ate lunch together and then walked

"You Can't Have the Green Card"

over to the Baltimore Aquarium—a fantastic structure that we thoroughly enjoyed strolling through. With aquatic life all around us, we talked to Charlotte and got to know more about the Hearn family, especially her father Charles and my wife's grandfather Samuel, who had been called S.E. Jr. by his family. We learned that Charlotte had known her uncle quite well, as he had frequented her childhood home. We also learned that Samuel had never really gotten control of his drinking, which eventually led to liver damage and his untimely demise.

Although that part of the story was saddening, we were pleased to learn more about a past that had been so vague during my wife's upbringing.

We also learned more about Charlotte, who had married a Navy officer named Tony Reid and together they had two grown boys, Charles and Joel, both of whom we have had the pleasure to meet and spend time with since.

When we drove from Baltimore, we felt a *sense of relief.* All our interactions with Charlotte had been pleasantly familiar.

Driving back to Ocean City that day I learned that is not always a good idea to follow GPS directions blindly. That day the navigation system directed us through some rather shady neighborhoods in Baltimore. We kept our doors locked and emerged unscathed. It was a good lesson.

While our current residence in Austin is very safe, I have developed a heightened sense of alertness since we moved from the sheltered shores of Iceland. There, acts of extreme violence are so rare, that when the police shot a man to death for the first time in Icelandic history, in the fall of 2013, they apologized.

* * *

More emotional rollercoasters awaited us when we arrived in Texas. My mother's friend Sharon Watkins — whom she had met at her Hotel Hellnar while Sharon stayed there on her travels around Iceland several years earlier — picked us up at the Austin airport.

During our drive to San Marcos, Johanna and I talked almost constantly about how Texas was not at all how we had *imagined* it. In our minds, we were going into an area with deserts, cactuses, and cowboy hats. Instead, Texas had lush fields, green trees, vast blue skies and we *didn't see a single cowboy hat*. The only thing that was true about what we had heard prior to arriving was that Texas

"You Can't Have the Green Card"

was scorching hot. Speaking to that, our preconceptions have been challenged a number of times since we moved here. Sometimes the stereotypes have turned out to be accurate, but more often than not our assumptions have been wrong. As everyone who has travelled can attest to, it can be quite misleading to form opinions about a society based on news media and television shows that are written for entertainment. In our case, weeding reality from erroneous preconceptions has been an interesting learning process.

When we finally arrived at the apartment complex in San Marcos on a Friday afternoon, we learned that the furniture we had arranged to rent prior to our arrival had been turned away earlier that day because we had not yet signed the apartment lease. That was in clear contradiction to what we had been told over the phone, and meant that we would not be getting any furniture until Monday at the earliest. Because most of the hotels in San Marcos were booked that weekend, and because we didn't have a rental car yet, we decided to stay in the empty apartment.

Fortunately, Sharon was with us and we scrambled to buy inflatable mattresses, food, and simple plastic utensils. I stayed in the apartment with my daughter while Johanna, Sharon and Daniel ran the errands. They brought back burgers, fries and sodas for dinner. Being a restaurant owner, Sharon had not eaten fast food for years, so when she was asked if she wanted to buy a large drink at Jack in the Box, she said yes. When the three of them arrived with the food and drinks at the apartment, we couldn't stop laughing at the half-gallon sized soda containers. "Who drinks this?" we took turns exclaiming. We haven't ordered a large soda since.

When Sharon had left and the kids were asleep, Johanna and I sat on the floor, physically and emotionally exhausted after a long day of travel and problem solving. In a quiet moment, sitting on the bare white carpet, listening to romantic music on the radio we had brought with us from Iceland, we enjoyed a slice of the Lemon Rosemary Cake that Sharon had brought us from her restaurant in Austin. Each bite was absolutely delicious and a welcome reward after the day's misfortunes.

With only two air mattresses, the four of us camped out on the floor in the empty third floor apartment for three nights and made the best of our situation. The kids thoroughly enjoyed the camping element and had great fun playing

"You Can't Have the Green Card"

around in the wide open spaces of the empty apartment.

The day after we arrived, I had made plans to walk to the rental car agency, which was within a 30 minute walking distance according to Google Maps. Fortunately, the apartment manager talked me out of walking and instead called the agency and had them pick me up. When I drove the route, I realized my folly. There were no sidewalks and the temperature was well over 100° Fahrenheit, which is about 40° Celsius (I kept making the conversion from Fahrenheit to Celsius for the first few months, but soon gave up and only use Fahrenheit now… you know, "when in Rome…"). This lack of sidewalks is a phenomenon that I have encountered both in Florida and all around Texas. I have repeatedly gone on walks and then either had to walk through tall grass or turn around whenever a sidewalk has mysteriously disappeared. It was a good thing that I didn't walk that day, as I could have easily become dehydrated, lost my way, or both. This was underscored by the rental car guy, who, during our ride to the agency, asked me over and over again in an incredulous tone: "You were *really* going to *walk*?"

Emotional Rollercoasters

Soon after we arrived in San Marcos we planned a trip to Houston to meet Cindy, Charlotte's sister, and her family. During the three hour drive to Houston, my wife went through another emotional rollercoaster, wondering how our second encounter with the family would turn out, but once we met Cindy, it was just as familiar as when we met Charlotte. As I use the word *familiar* a second time, a word which kept coming up during our interactions with the Hearn family, I decided to look it up in the dictionary. One of the definitions was "relating to or involving family."

On our first day in Houston, Cindy drove us around and showed us the courtroom where her father, the honorable judge Charles J. Hearn, had presided over the 263rd State District Court. The courtroom was in a skyscraper situated near the city center. That part of the trip was exciting, because none of us had ever been inside a courtroom before. In addition to seeing the inside of a courtroom we also got an excellent view of the city from the 15th floor.

We then visited the grave of my wife's grandfather, the late Samuel Emmett Hearn Jr., amid thousands of other tombstones in a veteran's cemetery in Houston. Visiting his grave was truly

"You Can't Have the Green Card"

one of the highlights of our trip. Through a hue of tears, standing over her grandfather's grave, Johanna found closure.

Cindy's son, Lukas, accompanied us on the daytrip, while her husband, Russell, was working. Later, we got to know Russ well when he took me and Daniel to our first baseball game where the Phillies played the Astros. Russ had never met anyone who didn't know baseball, so he talked almost non-stop for three hours, explaining every detail of the game. We enjoyed ourselves immensely, and as fortune would have it, the Astros actually won that day. Russ did a great job of explaining the intricacies of the game. Thanks to him I became interested in baseball and even watched the postseason for the first time that fall — when the Yankees won the World Series.

During our trip to Houston, we also had the pleasure of meeting Carrie, Charlotte's and Cindy's mother, who had asked her friend to convey the news of Samuel's passing back in 1981. Up until that point in our journey, Carrie was the only one we had met who actually remembered Johanna senior and Jo Ann from all those years ago. Married to the Hearn brothers, Carrie and Johanna senior had been very close during Johanna's fourteen year stay in Texas.

My wife sat and talked to Carrie into the night—long after I left for the hotel with our kids. She was intent on learning as much as she could about her grandmother's time in the USA. When Johanna got back to the hotel that night, she talked about how similar Carrie and her grandmother were in many ways. Both were extremely thin and heavy smokers, both had an air of calm and toughness about them, and both were quick to make a joke. She told me that when Carrie and Charles had divorced, Charles had remarried and dedicated much of his life to community service. Carrie had also remarried and had been widowed. Even though her health was failing, she was in high spirits.

*   *   *

Once we were back in San Marcos, it was time for school to start, both for my wife and my son. I will never forget his first day of school because thinking about it still makes my stomach churn. We had registered Daniel as a car rider at school, but when I came to pick him up in the car lane that

"You Can't Have the Green Card"

first day, he was nowhere to be found. Within ten minutes of utter confusion, it was evident that he was not at school. The feeling of not knowing where my son was located—fearing the worst—having heard all the crazy stories about child abductions in the USA—was almost more than I could bear. After approximately thirty minutes of not knowing where he was, I was as close to losing my mind as I have ever been. I was nearly brought to tears.

It turned out that he had been mislabeled as a walker and was happily walking home while I was losing my mind in the parking lot. We didn't have a mobile phone at the time, so when my wife heard a knock on the door and saw my son standing there alone, she scrambled to find a phone and call the school. I have never been as happy to see him as I was when I arrived at the apartment. I hugged him tightly with a lump in my throat.

Moments later, his teacher, a young woman who had just finished her first day of teaching, showed up at the door in tears, just to make sure he was all right. She was visibly shaken.

The upside to this very unpleasant episode was that after his first day of school *everyone* at Irene K.

Emotional Rollercoasters

Mendez Elementary in San Marcos knew who Daniel Bergmann was.

One week after school started, Daniel came home crying. He said that he didn't understand anything that the other kids were saying. We knew that he didn't know much English when we arrived, but we thought he knew enough to get along and were confident that he would pick it up quickly. When we went to investigate what was happening, we discovered that because we had marked a box when we filled out the paperwork that said we spoke a language other than English at home, he had been ascribed to a *bi-lingual* class. Furthermore, we learned that Spanish was the primary language in that bi-lingual class — because most of the kids spoke no English at all. No wonder he couldn't understand anything. After signing a disclaimer, Daniel was reassigned to a class where English was the primary language. By the time we headed for Iceland in December he was a near fluent English speaker.

*   *   *

Soon after school started in San Marcos, we were invited to meet more people from the Hearn family in Port Arthur on Labor Day weekend. In a

"You Can't Have the Green Card"

blue collar oil processing area, where towering industrial plants define much of the landscape, producing oil byproducts under household names such as Du Pont and Good Year, we met at the home of one my wife's oldest cousin. There were about 35 people there that Saturday, and many of them had not seen each other for over twenty years. The arrival of our small family unit from Iceland had created an unexpected family reunion.

Of all the people we met that day, one person stands out. Patricia Andrews Budd looked so much like my wife's mother Jo Ann when we met her that we could hardly believe it. We learned that Patsy, as she is known to the family, and Jo Ann, had been inseparable when they were kids. Patsy talked about how she used to carry Jo Ann around on her hip. When Jo Ann moved to Iceland at the age of six both Patsy and her mother Mary, who was Samuel's sister, were distraught. Patsy had wondered ever since what had become of Jo Ann and was overjoyed to meet us.

When we were on our way back from Port Arthur after the reunion, I turned to my wife and said: "We have to bring your mother here for Thanksgiving. Most of these people are old, and there is no guarantee that they will be alive if we

Emotional Rollercoasters

wait for your mother to make a trip on her own in a year or two." My wife agreed.

After convincing Jo Ann that she had to visit us in San Marcos that fall, we bought her an airplane ticket with accumulated airline miles. In addition to our contribution, my wife's brother and sister pitched in, and so did my mother Runa — who has been more than generous in her support of our move here. The stage was set for yet another family reunion.

And so it came to pass, that after having left the country of her birth at the age of six, my mother-in-law Jo Ann Hearn, returned to the USA in November of 2009, exactly *fifty years* after she had moved to Iceland.

My mother, Runa, and my wife's sister, Thury, also came to visit — my mother had planned to visit us well before we convinced Jo Ann to come, but my wife's younger sister had to make her decision in haste. As she had been involved in the reunion of the two families from the beginning, she jumped at the opportunity to meet everyone.

The seven of us, two grandmothers, two sisters, two kids, and me, all stayed together in our two bedroom apartment in San Marcos prior to going to Houston for our first Thanksgiving.

"You Can't Have the Green Card"

That year we had a double Thanksgiving celebration with Cindy and Russ at their apartment complex clubhouse—first with their mother's side of the family for Thanksgiving, and then with the Hearn family who gathered to meet Jo Ann and Thury on the Saturday after Thanksgiving.

Jo Ann was thrilled to meet her relatives and completely overwhelmed by all the outpouring of love and acceptance. As an *only child*, she had never had a big family. All of a sudden there were dozens of people welcoming her as one of their own. It was truly a joy to watch. As expected, Jo Ann and Patsy, who had been inseparable during childhood, created an immediate bond. They have continued to strengthen their relationship, and I am glad to report that the two of them speak almost daily on Skype. My mother-in-law is even teaching Patsy how to *crochet* over the internet.

*   *   *

In hindsight I can say that the process of reconnecting with the Hearn family in the USA went much better than any of us could have expected. Today, we mostly stay in touch with Cindy, Charlotte and Patsy, but get to meet more distant cousins on a regular basis, and the feeling is always one of familiarity and comfort. The saying "a cousin of a cousin is a cousin of mine" has truly been honored in our case, because even without blood relations to Cindy and Charlotte's mother's side of the family we have absolutely been treated like a part of their family ever since that first Thanksgiving.

When I celebrated my citizenship at the beginning of November in 2013, four of Johanna's cousins drove all the way from Houston to Austin to join in the celebration. As a present for the occasion Cindy brought us a sign that says *Families are Forever*. It currently hangs above our fireplace.

—Chapter 5—

Pointing at the Map

On July 1ˢᵗ, 2010, we boarded an airplane headed for New York. It seemed unreal at the time, but we were moving – permanently. I was armed with my green card and my wife and kids had valid U.S. passports.

When we stayed in San Marcos during the fall of 2009, we were introduced to U.S. and Texan culture and took care of some basic things, such as getting Social Security numbers for every family member and opening a bank account. We visited Austin, toured the State Capitol, and saw the famous Congress Bridge bats, millions of which fly into the night sky at sunset. We also visited San Antonio, toured the Alamo, the beautiful River Walk, and took in a Spurs basketball game. But mostly we enjoyed the small town feel of San Marcos and the close by town of Wimberley (the sweet potato fries and chipotle ranch dressing at

"You Can't Have the Green Card"

the diner on the main square in Wimberley are well worth the trip).

While Daniel and Johanna went to school, I stayed at home with my then one year old daughter, Hanna, and used the time to write my tenth book, while also subconsciously learning a number of theme songs from children's TV shows and frequenting parks and play areas in the neighborhood.

During our stay in San Marcos, we often talked about *where* we should move once my wife finished her studies at Reykjavik University the following summer. We were determined to move from Iceland to the USA and all options were on the table. Still, when we returned to Iceland in December of 2009 we had only narrowed our options down to the East Coast, the West Coast, and Texas, if that counts as narrowing. We had no idea of where we were going to move — we only knew that we were moving.

People often ask us why we moved from Iceland. We don't have crystal clear answers to that question. Our reasons were part adventurism, part "we have to check it out since we got this opportunity," part "we don't know," part the Icelandic economy, and part the unpredictable Icelandic weather. While the natural surroundings in Iceland are exceptionally beautiful during certain times of the year, there are long bouts of sideways rain, sleet, snow, and over four months of darkness (very short days and long nights). Northern States in the USA, such as Minnesota and Illinois, are colder than Iceland, but the unpredictability of weather in Iceland can be quite taxing. That being said, there are things we miss about Iceland in addition to our family, like the ocean, the mountains, the warm swimming pools, the hot tubs and the ability to see for miles in any direction.

*   *   *

We arrived in Iceland just in time for Christmas in 2009, but once January of 2010 came around, everything shifted into high gear. That spring, four of Johanna's cousins came to visit from the USA, Patsy, Charlotte, Nancy and Michelle; the infamous Eyjafjallajokull erupted in Iceland, disrupting air traffic all over Europe; Johanna finished her master's degree in international business; I wrapped up my business, and we sold most of our stuff. In hindsight those months were fast paced

"You Can't Have the Green Card"

and blurry — yet, they were also filled with promise and excitement.

Although our self-proclaimed moving date in July 2010 was fast approaching, it wasn't until April that same year that we decided where we were moving. After months of deliberation, we ended up choosing Austin, Texas as our destination. Based on our brief visits to Austin, the city had a warm aura about it. However, we did not know the area well and were not moving there for work. The deciding factors were neither this nor that. When people ask us why we moved to Austin we can truthfully answer: "We pointed at the map."

The upside of choosing Austin was that the city was close to many of Johanna's new found relatives, who lived in Houston and Nederland. The downside was that we only knew one person there — the aforementioned Sharon Watkins, my mother's friend, who ended up playing a pivotal role once we arrived.

As soon as we had chosen our destination, we bought one way airplane tickets for the first time in our lives and started looking for a place to live. Based on a number of criteria, including school ratings and crime statistics, we chose North West

Austin as our final destination — without ever having been there. I can't tell you how many hours I spent researching the NW area online, trying to imagine what it would be like to live there. What I can tell you is that we chose a good area. We loved the elementary school, Forest North Elementary, which both of our children attended, and we were centrally located with good access to downtown Austin, the nearby Lake Travis, outdoor areas in Cedar Park, Leander, and Round Rock, and toll ways that gave us easy access to the airport.

*   *   *

Prior to leaving Iceland we went through an emotional graduation and farewell party. While we interacted with our friends and family during the party we talked like we would be able to visit Iceland on a regular basis. That has not been the case. I have been back to Iceland twice for work, my children have visited once, and my wife has not been able to visit at all. We did not fully realize what it meant to make a permanent move prior to our departure. Now we do. Austin is far away from Iceland. Most of our friends who have left Iceland have moved to Norway, Denmark or the

"You Can't Have the Green Card"

United Kingdom, and they visit their families on a regular basis. While we are overall happy with our decision, we still miss our family and would like to see them more often. We would especially like them to see our children with more regularity, as the two of them are growing up so fast. Thankfully, my mom has come to visit us more than ten times since we moved, and Skype and Facebook have allowed us to stay connected in a way that was previously impossible. We often think about how isolated Johanna senior must have been while she lived in Texas in the 40's and 50's. At that time, she only talked to her family on the phone once or twice a year. We, on the other hand, sometimes contact our family in Iceland on a daily basis.

After the farewell party, we packed what was left of our belongings on two pallets and sent them on a cross Atlantic trip. You know how people say that they have a *ton of stuff*? Well, that's literally how much we had. The pictures, books, and other personal belongings that we decided to bring along weighed roughly one ton.

*   *   *

On July 1st, 2010, we boarded an airplane headed for New York. It seemed unreal at the time, but we were moving — permanently. I was armed with my green card and my wife and kids had valid U.S. passports. We stayed in New York overnight before continuing on to Austin. Our first day in the States without return tickets was spent travelling to Times Square in New York, where we dined at Planet Hollywood and visited a multi-story Toys 'R Us store. Although the trip was memorable and made a good story, I felt that New York was loud, crowded and unappealing. I may have a different view if I ever go there on an adult only trip, but because we were travelling with our kids — a two year old and a seven year old — my protective urges were in overdrive.

On July 2^{nd,} we arrived in Austin. Our feeling, when we arrived at Bergstrom International airport, was one of comfort and ease. In contrast to JFK, the Austin airport was calm and the surroundings, which emphasized Austin as the live music capitol of the world, were quite charming.

We were picked up at the airport by Kristel Gonzaba, a girl in her twenties whom we had met when we were in San Marcos in 2009. She became a friend of the family when she stayed as an exchange student in Iceland in the spring of 2010. We packed all our stuff, about six suitcases and several

"You Can't Have the Green Card"

carry-on items, into Kirstel's SUV and she drove us to Presidio Apartments — the apartment complex in NW Austin where we would live for the next two and a half years.

While we were signing the rental agreement, it rained so heavily that we wondered if the entire Gulf of Mexico was descending upon us. I picked up our rental car during that period of heavy rain and nearly got lost on the way back to the apartment complex. While the weather in Texas is mostly hot, it can also be summarized as draught with a chance of flooding. When it rains, it pours.

*   *   *

It took us a little over two weeks to get settled in, which meant buying furniture and necessary electrical appliances. Unlike our experience in San Marcos, this time we knew we would be moving into an empty apartment and would again need inflatable mattresses. To begin with, those air mattresses were used for sleeping, until we got beds. Then, they served as adequate seating arrangements, until we got a sofa. Now, they are used as guest beds whenever people come to stay with us.

Pointing at the Map

Once the two pallets with our belongings arrived from Iceland, I carried our literal ton of stuff from the ground floor to our third floor apartment. It was quite a workout.

Because we had no credit history in the USA, I could only buy a car for cash. With little car buying experience, I got a good deal on a Mercury Grand Marquis 2001. I still own that car. It has a V8 engine and has been driven about 154,000 miles at this point. In Iceland, I would never have bought a car like the Mercury for two reasons. Firstly, it guzzles too much gas and gasoline in Iceland is very expensive. Secondly, it wouldn't have gotten me around during the winter in Iceland with its rear wheel drive and heavy frame. With icing on the road, I would have been skidding around uncontrollably. That being said, I love that car and love being able to drive it all year round.

Recently I realized that I must have played out a subconscious fantasy when I bought the Mercury. The frame of my car is almost identical to the classic Ford Crown Victoria police cars I was accustomed to seeing on my favorite TV shows as a kid. Watching American TV when I was growing up most likely sowed the seeds for that purchase.

"You Can't Have the Green Card"

In addition to furnishing our apartment and purchasing necessities, we also needed to get used to the weather again. We had gotten a taste of the heat during our previous year in San Marcos, but there is a stark difference between visiting an area and living there. During our first three months at Presidio, we spent an enormous amount of time at the community pool, soaking up the sun. But since then we have completely changed our relationship with the sun. We now park our car in the shade and are always armed with sunscreen. In Iceland, we used to run out and take our clothes off any time the sun came out—now we stay in the shade and are mostly active at dawn and dusk during the hottest months.

To give you an example of the sun worshipping mentality in Iceland I can tell you that when I visited Iceland in 2012 the first words out of my wife's aging aunt were not "Hello" or "How are you?" as one would expect. Instead, she shook my hand, looked me in the eye and said: "You're *not tan at all*." She expected that I would be dark skinned after living in sun soaked Texas for a couple of years.

Although it is true that the heat can be quite daunting during the middle of summer in Austin, we have found that 8-9 months out of the year the weather here is almost perfect.

We did our best to acclimatize in the fall of 2010, both to the weather and the culture, but we soon realized that living in Austin was not all sunshine and lollypops.

Prior to moving, I had been the main provider for the family while Johanna attended university from 2005 to 2010. We had decided to switch places when we moved. She was going to look for a job sporting her brand new master's degree in international business, while I was going to build my speaking and writing career while also staying at home with the kids. With 20/20 hindsight it is clear that our goals were unrealistic at best. Our circumstances became a lot more challenging than we anticipated.

—Chapter 6—

Challenging Times

Reflecting on these challenging times, it seems to me that when our situation has gotten really bad, something positive has always materialized.

Up to this point in our story, it certainly seemed like some unseen force had been conspiring to get us to the States. Leading up to our departure from Iceland everything seemed to go our way. We must have expected that trend to continue, because when we arrived in Austin we were exceedingly hopeful.

Johanna had a newly minted master's degree, and I had spent the previous ten years honing my skills as an author, yoga teacher and speaker — travelling to America and England on a regular basis, attending trainings with a variety of teachers and trainers, putting their ideas to work in Iceland with good results. While Johanna attended univer-

"You Can't Have the Green Card"

sity in Iceland, I was making a good income and provided for all our needs. I naively thought I could replicate my success from Iceland once we were in the States. I spoke English as well as any native and was equipped with a marketing and motivational toolbox that had proven to be fruitful in Iceland.

However, contrary to our expectations, neither my previous expertise nor Johanna's new degree made an immediate impact on the Austin market. Johanna did all that she could during her job hunt, but as we edged closer to Christmas 2010 with no apparent job openings, not even an interview in sight, and with our savings almost depleted, we started *seriously doubting* our decision to move. That fall, Johanna donned a white shirt and started waiting tables during the occasional banquet at Chez Zee, the restaurant that our friend Sharon Watkins owned. In addition, she also worked temporarily as Sharon's assistant.

It became apparent by the middle of January 2011 that our situation was dire. We had no money left in our savings account and were dependent upon my mother for the first time in our adult lives, who fortunately was able to support us financially through the most difficult periods.

Challenging Times

That year, for the first time in my life, I uncharacteristically went through several periods of gloom and melancholy. It was as close as I have come to being depressed. In hindsight I can say that 2011 was the most trying year of my life thus far — and the effects still linger.

*   *   *

In February, after seven months of continuous job hunting, Johanna finally got her first fulltime job in the USA. She was hired as an account manager with a lead generation company, but in retrospect there were warning signs from the beginning. The interview was done over the phone, and the company did not complete a background check — both of which we now recognize as signs of an unprofessional hiring process.

When that job didn't last, we tried for a while to build a stress management business around my expertise. I got one gig as a keynote speaker at a large leadership conference in August (which paid rather handsomely), but when I reflect on the impact that one booking had, I can safely say that it gave us false hope and kept both of us from exploring other avenues of income.

"You Can't Have the Green Card"

When it was clear, in the fall of 2011, that the stress management business would not support us, Johanna again got a job with Sharon as an event manager at Chez Zee. She got the job because she was present when the previous event manager quit, and immediately offered to fill the vacancy.

I stayed at home with our children as we had decided and did what I could to advance — writing books and creating contacts. I'll admit that my preconceptions about what it would be like to be a stay-at-home-dad were completely off the mark. I went from being insanely busy, to caring for a two year old all day — a necessary job, but much less demanding. When I think about the biggest difference between working full-time and staying at home, I have to say that it is the visible output. When I worked, I saw results, but at home I could do the same thing over and over again without seeing much difference. Cooking and cleaning is like Buddhist *mandala* making (displayed by monks who create elaborate pictures with colored sand and then sweep them away to remind themselves of the transient nature of the world). I firmly agree with my mother-in-law who says that even though no one seems to notice what the person staying at home is doing, everyone notices if she doesn't do it. My appreciation for stay-at-home parents has skyrocketed based on my experiences, and I am glad to say that the role of stay-at-home-dad has grown on me.

As an event manager at Chez Zee, Johanna got to meet a number of very interesting people, and the job kept her busy beyond belief. However, in the back of her mind she couldn't help thinking that this wasn't exactly her dream job—not what she had spent five years in university to prepare for.

Consequently, it seemed fortunate when she met the owner of a company in 2012 that she had interviewed with in 2011. As luck would have it, they met at the restaurant where Johanna was working. He was having lunch, called her over, and asked if she was still interested. After a follow up meeting he offered her a job as his marketing director. Along with that new position Johanna got a pay raise, which made our lives more comfortable. She poured her heart and soul into that job. For a while, everything seemed to be going her way, but regrettably the situation was more complicated than it seemed to be in the beginning. As a result, we hit yet another bump in the road when Johanna was let go without notice or cause in July 2013. To

"You Can't Have the Green Card"

add injury to insult, her boss tried to prevent her from getting unemployment benefits, which completely blindsided both of us.

We have found that the job market in Texas is much tougher than in Iceland. While I don't agree with all the rules and regulations in Iceland, by comparison the shortest grace period there is one month, and people usually have three months to find a new job. Here, the two week notice isn't even mandatory.

*   *   *

July and August in 2013 were crazy months. We scrambled and reached out to everyone we knew. Our cash situation was negative and by my calculations we didn't have much time to make things work. We were in a bind. By the middle of August 2013, we were as close to packing our bags and moving back to Iceland as we have ever been.

Reflecting on these challenges, it seems to me that when our situation has gotten really bad something positive has always materialized. Our periods of desperation have been disrupted with rays of hope, thus far.

Our most recent ray of hope appeared in late August 2013, when my wife was offered the best job opportunity of her career — an opportunity that she would not have gotten without her previous job as marketing director. She is finally in a job where she can fully employ her education and experience.

I, on the other hand, haven't found a way to create reliable streams of income with my considerable set of skills. Since we moved here, I have written and produced eleven books, started a stress management company, a book consulting business, taught yoga at various locations, and even took a stab at running a yoga studio for a few months. I have done all that in addition to cooking, cleaning and being the primary caretaker at home.

Being busy is nothing new for me, as I have always juggled a number of different projects at any given time. However, during the past three years I have often felt like I was stuck inside a *hamster wheel*, continually working without making much progress. It's hard to stay motivated when the output prompts little or no response. If it weren't for my wife, who has continued to believe in my abilities and support the family financially, I would probably have abandoned my dreams much earlier in the process. That being said, it may be time for me to reinvent myself. The future is a blank canvas and I have not decided what to paint yet.

*   *   *

Although our challenges periodically seemed insurmountable, I see several things to be grateful for. I have been well received whenever I have had the chance to show what I can do in the areas of teaching, training and consulting. I have gotten better at writing in English, even though my books haven't sold in truckloads. I have become quite skillful at networking. I know from experience that I will continue to function in the face of adversity, and best of all, I have developed a strong relationship with my children, something for which I am eternally grateful.

Over the past three years, dealing with these unforeseen challenges, Johanna and I have learned that there is a thin line between synchronous events on the one hand, where everything seems to flow effortlessly, and everyday realities on the other hand, where struggle is the norm. In hindsight, we should have been better prepared, but then again, we probably wouldn't have moved here if we had known in advance everything we had to go through. Discovering the perils and pleasures on the road ahead means that one has to travel down that road—and that is exactly what we have done.

—Chapter 7—

Network of Supportive Friends

To add an element of synchronicity and to demonstrate how small Iceland really is, we soon found out that Stefan's older sister Sirry worked in my childhood home – looking after my younger brother and me when I was in my teens.

The challenges described in the previous chapter would have been even more trying, had it not been for the group of friends and acquaintances we have made since we moved here. That group didn't just materialize out of thin air. Anyone who has ever moved to a new country, or even to a new city, knows that making friends when you are an adult is not as easy as it sounds. After we moved we realized that we had to be *proactive* and reach out to the community around us if we were to make new friends. When we thought about how to approach that unfamiliar undertaking, we realized

"You Can't Have the Green Card"

that there were approximately four ways to connect with new people.

One, we could meet through proximity — our neighbors, co-workers, kids friends, etc.

Two, we could reach out to the Icelandic community in Austin.

Three, we could go to networking events.

Four, we could join a church — something we had repeatedly been advised to do prior to leaving Iceland.

While we initially resisted going to church (as I will explain later), we have done *all of the above* with good results. The following are examples of how we met some of the people that are now in our circle of friends.

*   *   *

Only two days after we arrived in Austin, our friend Sharon Watkins invited us to a 4th of July brunch at her restaurant and introduced us to a lovely family — an elderly couple, Alek and Irmina, who are immigrants from Poland, their son-in-law Chris, and their grandson Alek. Over a delicious brunch — which is the Chez Zee specialty — Sharon told us that she had been the first person Irmina had met when she came to the States thirty years prior. Although we had just arrived, it was interesting to compare immigration stories. On the face of it, our stories couldn't have been more different. Escaping from Communist controlled Poland on one hand and finding out that one had been a U.S. citizen from birth on the other hand seemed like *polar opposites*—that is, until one entertained the historical fact that both the Communist takeover of Poland and my wife's relationship to the USA could be traced back to World War II.

As it turned out, Chris and his wife Karina (Alek and Irmina's daughter, who we got to meet later) were our age and fun to be around. They soon invited us into their home and introduced us to the rest of their family. We watched the World Cup final in soccer with them that summer, and soon thereafter Alek senior took us out on Lake Travis on his boat. We are forever grateful to them for making us feel welcomed so soon after we arrived.

*   *   *

In October 2010, we made first contact with the Icelandic community in Austin. A friend of mine

"You Can't Have the Green Card"

from Iceland, Birgir, connected me with his friend, Stefan, who had lived in Austin for years. We met Stefan and Sonia Stefansson (which is an example of how "the son of" tradition in Iceland turns into a last name in the USA) for the first time on a beautiful fall day. We were invited to their children's elementary school during the fall fair.

Stefan and Sonia, who met when Stefan was studying at the University of Texas in the 90's, have been welcoming beyond belief. They have introduced us to the entire Icelandic community in Austin—a little over twenty people—including Olof, who became one of my wife's best friends, and Maja, who has become our good friend and a substitute grandmother to our children. They have further invited us to spend the holidays with them. When we attended Christmas Day lunch at their house in 2013, which was our fourth time celebrating Christmas at their house, I realized that Sri Lankan curry—Sonia is originally from Sri Lanka, but moved to the States when she was eight—has become a new traditional taste of Christmas for me (*who would have thought*).

Stefan, Sonia, and their children have truly become our family away from home. To add an element of synchronicity and to demonstrate how small Iceland really is, we soon found out that Stefan's older sister Sirry had worked in my childhood home— looking after my younger brother and me when I was in my teens.

There is something strangely comforting about socializing with other Icelandic people. In addition to sharing a language and having a similar background, our barren island in the north seems to consistently produce a dry wit and refreshingly direct communications.

*   *   *

When it came to networking, I drew a blank. I had never networked in Iceland—simply because everyone knew everyone else (there are two degrees of separation in Iceland, not the better known six degrees). To make up for my years of deficiency on the subject, I did what I always do—I bought a few books and studied. Soon thereafter, I started going to events armed with business cards and a smile. I went to established networking events, such as the Metropolitan Breakfast Club, while also searching out smaller events and booking private meetings. Through my networking efforts, I have learned that less is more. Focusing on making stronger connections with fewer people has been much more effective than trying to distribute as many business cards as I possibly can.

In addition to venturing out, I made a number of acquaintances through LinkedIn. In one attempt to connect, I sent a personal letter to about two dozen men who I imagined might have something in common with me based on their profiles. The letter was of a personal nature and described some of the things I was interested in and highlighted the authors I was into at the time.

The LinkedIn Letter

Greetings!

This is not a business email. I decided to put together some information about myself and have chosen a handful of men I want to connect with. You are one of them. If you see similarities between us then please contact me. If not, then simply delete this email, no hard feelings.

I moved from Iceland, where I was born in 1972, to Austin on July 2nd last year with my family – my wife Johanna and two kids, Daniel and Hanna. We found out in 2009 that my wife had been a U.S. citi-

Network of Supportive Friends

zen from birth (long story) and we decided to go for it. We sold all our stuff in Iceland and simply pointed at the map ... "let's go here". Johanna and I have been happily married since 2001.

In Iceland, I was a chameleon of sorts and semi-famous. I owned a yoga studio for several years, wrote and published a number of books, worked on TV and radio, wrote articles for newspapers, was a highly paid motivational speaker, and much more. In Austin, I founded Austin Stress Management in January this year and just published my fourteenth book titled "Yes! You Can Manage Stress".

I play the guitar and sing. I wanted to be an actor in my early twenties and played the lead role in a few musicals, including Rocky Horror and Grease. I used to be a music critic and like all kinds of good music, especially seventies rock, mantra chanting, jazz, world music, classical music, and even disco – to name a few.

I have read hundreds of books in the past fifteen years. My all-time favorite author is the philosopher Ken Wilber. I have read most of his books more than once. Other favorite non-fiction authors are Wayne Dyer, Dan Millman, Susan Jeffers, Viktor Frankl,

"You Can't Have the Green Card"

M. Scott Peck, Brian Tracy, Seth Godin, Joseph Campbell, Gandhi, Yogi Shanti Desai, Will Durant and Napoleon Hill. I have also read a lot of Eastern and Greek philosophy. Favorite fiction authors are Kurt Vonnegut, Frank Herbert, Robert Heinlein, Herman Hesse and Jerzy Kosinski. I was in a book club in Iceland where we read one book a month and discussed the content. I would really like to get something similar going in Austin.

Politically I am a free thinker, agree with both sides on a number of issues and would be considered an independent if pressed for it.

As I said at the beginning of this email, I am looking to make likeminded friends and acquaintances. If you feel like we could make a connection, please let me know.

Sincerely,

Gudjon Bergmann

Only a few of the men replied. Nevertheless, I considered the venture a great success because three of them became good friends of mine.

Network of Supportive Friends

For one particular encounter, I had to travel all the way to Los Angeles. At a James Malinchak event in 2011, at the Westin Hotel near the LA airport, I met Annette Maxberry-Carrara — a fellow author and publisher, who also lived in Austin. We became fast friends. Soon thereafter I introduced her to my wife and children, and we got to know her husband Jean-Louis and their two adult children. The families bonded and have met on a number of occasions. When we later found out that Annette had been ordained as an interfaith minister, we asked her to perform the ceremony when Johanna and I got remarried on our eleventh wedding anniversary in 2012.

I'd like to underline the fact that we remarried without getting divorced first. We mainly did it because laws in Iceland prevented Johanna from taking the Bergmann name when we first got married in 2001, although she wanted to do it for practical reasons. The laws there state that any person born in Iceland must relate their surname (if they have one) to either their mother or father. When we looked into it, getting married again was both easier and cheaper than going before a judge in Texas with our Icelandic papers to petition for a name change. In addition, we must admit that getting married again was more fun than simply renewing our vows and a great excuse to throw a party.

*   *   *

Finding a church to belong to was another matter altogether. Although we had been advised to join a church a number of times prior to leaving Iceland (as the fastest way to join a community), we resisted. In our minds, church was an out-of-date government run establishment where old people went for mass. The only times we went to church in Iceland was for weddings and funerals — and that was more for cultural reasons than spiritual ones. In Iceland, we had our group of friends and family, so there was little need for additional community, and we fulfilled our spiritual needs through New Age and yoga groups we associated with. My personal practice over the years has been one of non-denominational meditation and prayer.

We also resisted going to church in Texas, because both Johanna and I have a problem with religious fundamentalism. Both of us believe in a higher power, but in a trans-rational manner (a belief that transcends and includes reason). We felt the need for a spiritual community, but were unsure about how to venture out. What to do?

First we tried attending the local Unitarian Church in 2011, which I initially thought was a Unity Church—an organization I had read about while researching authors Louise Hay and Wayne Dyer years earlier. The Unitarian Church was nice, but they mostly focused on social justice and there was little emphasis on personal spiritual practices. I got to know the minister there fairly well. Unfortunately, it soon became clear that there were some divisions within the congregation. On top of that, we weren't making many friends there and the kids resisted the babysitting facility, so we stopped going.

Our need for a social gathering with spiritual connotations lingered.

The following year we discovered a society more to our liking at Unity Church of the Hills. I initially visited their grounds with my daughter in April 2012. As soon as I saw pictures of angels etched in the sidewalk—pictures which looked exactly like the ones on affirmation cards my mother had sold in her New Age store in Iceland in the nineties—I knew we had stumbled into familiar settings. The feeling was further confirmed when I noticed a Peace Pole from the World Peace Prayer Society on the grounds. I had belonged to that society in my early twenties. Their message is simply *May Peace Prevail on Earth* and I had erected several such poles in Iceland.

Once we attended our first service at Unity Church of the Hills—a service which didn't resemble any church service we had been to before—we knew that we had found a positive place to attend. At Unity, we encountered a diverse community of people—including spiritual seekers, agnostics, Christians, Buddhists, and even atheists—all coming together in the spirit of *oneness*.

The Reverend Stephen Bolen and his wife Mary have shown us genuine love and kindness and been warm and welcoming. They are truly a unique couple who spread love and light wherever they go. In addition, the music team at the church has been well worth our time and attention on Sunday mornings. Even though we don't show up for every Sunday service—as it is hard to teach old dogs new tricks and neither Johanna nor I were brought up in church going households—we have made a number of good friends there. At Unity people gather to remind each other that we are all children of God (*Universal Spirit* if you prefer). I principally agree with the philosophy of oneness. The community at Unity Church of the Hills is truly one of inclusion, non-judgment and acceptance.

Soon after we found Unity Church of the Hills, I started attending the Men's Fellowship Network meetings on Monday evenings. The group meets to discuss life, spirit and philosophy. I have an innate need to debate and the meetings provided an excellent discussion platform, with topics ranging from shallow and simple, to deep and profound. I have enjoyed the format and the company of the men who attend.

At my first fellowship meeting, the founder of the group, Clay Boykin, greeted me warmly. When I told him that I was from Iceland, he replied: "Oh, I know a woman from Iceland, who lives in Los Angeles."

I answered: "Her name wouldn't happen to be Runa?"

Clay's jaw almost dropped to the floor. "Yes!" he exclaimed.

As it turns out, we were talking about the same woman, a friend of my mother's, named Runa

Bouius—another example of how connected the world really is (and how small Iceland is).

That summer, Clay graciously invited me to the annual Men's Renewal, which was a two day getaway at Summers Mill—a ranch north of Austin. The renewal (I was told that the men in UCOH renew, they never retreat) was a place for men to discuss spiritual matters at a deeper level. I truly enjoyed the experience and bonded with several men during my two night stay at the ranch. Another man from the church, John Boyden, had asked me to speak at that renewal about my attempts to uncover the spirit within. After Reverend Stephen Bolen heard my talk, he asked me to fill in for him as a speaker at the church in December. I gladly accepted although I had never spoken at a church gathering before. That December in 2012, I spoke to the Unity congregation about forgiveness, which is a topic I have studied thoroughly and embraced over the years.

During the Monday night meeting after my first renewal, I was asked by the group to organize the next year's renewal—a task that I accepted and completed in the spring of 2013. I decided to hold the renewal at Radha Madhav Dham, the largest Hindu temple in the USA. The temple is housed in

Network of Supportive Friends

magnificent buildings on vast grounds with ceremonial areas, walking trails, and peacocks roaming around. The 2013 renewal was themed "Gathering of Truth" and included a variety of activities, from lectures to sharing circles, hiking to games, and meditation ceremonies to private interactions. Although the meals were strictly vegetarian (and really tasty), I got high praise from the group for organizing a trip to the world famous Salt Lick for finger licking BBQ. I am on track to organize part of the 2014 renewal as well.

* * *

On November 2nd, 2013, we celebrated my U.S. citizenship with a party and invited a number of people. Hosting a potluck is a custom that we have embraced since we moved to the USA, so we asked everyone to bring their favorite American dish to the party. Contributions included fried chicken, hot dogs, caramelized popcorn and sandwiches, but the comfort food of America was revealed, as more people brought *apple pies* than any other food.

In addition, a couple from the church, Lynn and Evelyn Green, brought me an American flag baseball cap, which I proudly wore during the party.

Today, our network of friends spreads far and wide. We have our Icelandic group, our group of friends from the church, our networking and business associates, our international friends, including people from India, France, Mexico, and Denmark, and of course, our current neighbors.

—Chapter 8—

Preserving Icelandic Heritage

Serving lamb is especially meaningful to me, because the last conversation I had with my father before he unexpectedly passed away on December 27th, 2004, was about how to prepare a leg of lamb, something which he was a master at.

Since we moved away from Iceland, we have struggled with what it means to preserve our Icelandic heritage. While language plays a crucial role, we have also found that food, folklore, and traditions continue to weigh in on our cultural preservation attempts.

We have made a conscious effort to blend in with U.S. society and have done our best to develop good English skills. Today, both Johanna and I communicate in English with ease, and our children speak English at native fluency levels, but we continue to speak Icelandic at home. Speaking

"You Can't Have the Green Card"

Icelandic comes naturally to me and Johanna because both of us have spoken that language from an early age. Nonetheless, we must admit that English slang has increasingly crept into our everyday communications, simply because everything outside of the home happens in English.

When I lived in Australia as an exchange student at the age of sixteen, I noticed that it took about three months of total immersion to start dreaming and thinking in English. When I returned to Iceland, I found it particularly difficult to tell stories about Australia. In my mind, everything had happened in English, not in Icelandic. Translating was difficult. I see the same thing happening with my children. Their school days happen in English. Therefore, it is very hard for them to come home from school and translate everything into Icelandic. Overall, it has been easier for our son, Daniel, to continue speaking Icelandic than it has been for our daughter, Hanna, who has spent most of her life here. He learned to speak, read and write while we still lived in Iceland, while she has never really gotten the kind exposure to the Icelandic language that one needs to learn it. We do our best. We read to her in Icelandic, teach her Icelandic songs, and speak to her in Icelandic at home, but she doesn't always reciprocate — sometimes she flat out refuses to speak in Icelandic. Without social surroundings, such as friends, teachers, and family, there is much less incentive to speak the language. In her defense, she makes more of an effort to speak Icelandic whenever either of her grandmothers comes to visit — both prior to their arrival, and while they are with us.

Although I am completely onboard with the idea that one needs to become proficient in the local language to blend in with society, I also understand the longing to preserve the language of the home country (even though most research shows that languages that are only spoken at home will all but disappear by the third generation of immigrants).

While it is a lot more difficult than we anticipated we will continue in our efforts to speak Icelandic at home. The Icelandic language carries with it a tremendous amount of history and culture, plus, our relatives in Iceland would never let it go if we didn't at least try to teach our children Icelandic. Speaking to my immigrant friends from other countries, I have noticed that such family pressure is an international phenomenon. Language is certainly a loaded subject matter.

"You Can't Have the Green Card"

Preserving traditions is another hot topic. Which traditions does one preserve and why? Let's take the holiday of Christmas for example. In Iceland, we honored the traditional folklore of the thirteen Yule Lads—who are said to make their way to town, one by one, every night, thirteen days before Christmas, each one bearing small gifts, such as candy, fruits or small toys, for kids who have been good. In Iceland, honoring the Yule Lads was a very important tradition to follow. But, after we moved to the States we were faced with the question: "Do the Yule Lads come to America?" We decided that they didn't, because we couldn't answer simple questions such as "How would they have made the trip?" and "What would the other kids at school say about our kids getting gifts every morning for thirteen days before Christmas?"

Another Christmas tradition we struggled with, was that in Iceland we opened the presents on Christmas Eve, but here, the tradition is to open the presents on the 25th. I selfishly opted for changing this tradition—mainly because my birthday is on the 24th of December. You see, Christmas Eve was a solemn occasion while I was growing up. When the clock struck 6 PM everyone was wearing their finest clothes. Church bells on the radio ushered in the holiday. After wishing each other "Merry Christmas", the family gathered at the table for dinner and presents were opened afterwards. Because of the sacred nature of this holiday it was all but impossible to fit a birthday party into the festivities while I was growing up, but to her credit, my mother always made sure that I had a birthday party prior to the Christmas celebrations when I was a kid.

Freeing up the 24th for my birthday celebrations has created a new tradition. We now spend the day engaging in family activities instead of preparing for Christmas Eve. In 2013, we stayed in our pajamas all day, watched *Yogi Bear's First Christmas*, a cartoon from my childhood years, played board games, baked cookies, listened to Christmas music, and feasted on a leg of lamb at dinner time. It was one of the best birthdays I have ever had. That's not all. As it turns out, we really like opening presents on the 25th. That way, the kids are energetic and excited, and have time to play with their toys and games for hours afterwards. Contrast that with kids in Iceland, who often wake up at 6 AM on the 24th and wait impatiently all day (usually to around 7 or 8 PM), to be able to start unwrapping their presents. Talk about tension and

"You Can't Have the Green Card"

excitement—especially with young kids. It's a situation that is apt to create a mental strain for even the most seasoned parents. We may return to traditional Icelandic celebrations on Christmas Eve as the kids grow older, but for now, we are happy with the changes we have made.

In addition to the folklore of the Yule Lads, Iceland has other interesting mythologies worth knowing about. Since we moved I have been invited to my son's classroom three times to talk about Icelandic Elves and Trolls. I have explained to the kids that in the olden days it probably didn't take much to imagine supernatural beings in Iceland during the dark months, especially in the picturesque lava landscape that often seems to be molded into Troll like shapes (and of course everyone *knows* that Trolls turn into stone once they see daylight). During each presentation I have received gasps, laughs, and a barrage of questions from students and teachers alike.

*   *   *

Of the few traditions that we do keep, most of them have to do with food. Every Icelandic person that has visited us thus far has brought with them either boatloads of Icelandic candy (for example, a special kind of licorice that you can't get anywhere else, or, Icelandic milk chocolate, which is some of the best in the world), or they have brought some kind of preserved meat, either a smoked leg of lamb (an Icelandic person travelling through JFK around Christmas will have a hard time convincing the customs inspector that they don't have any *Hangikjot* with them) or my son's favorite, Icelandic hot dogs.

To preserve a unique taste from home, I convinced my mother-in-law to teach me how to make thin traditional Icelandic pancakes prior to leaving Iceland. They resemble French crepes, but are smaller and are baked on specially made pans—of which I own two today (my oldest brother brags that he can bake on three pans simultaneously, while I have only mastered two at a time). These pancakes are usually served with either sugar or whipped cream and jam. Whenever I have made them, either at home or at potluck gatherings (they have to be made fresh and served immediately in my opinion), the pancakes have been exceptionally well received. Being able to create that unique taste from Iceland is something I treasure. I am grateful to my mother-in-law for teaching me the recipe and baking method before we left. My recipe

"You Can't Have the Green Card"

arsenal also includes my mother's buttercream chocolate cake, which was reserved for birthdays when I was growing up, and her cheese filled meatballs, which I have only recently mastered.

A year after we moved, we discovered that Whole Foods sells Icelandic lamb in the fall. Ever since, it has been a fall tradition to purchase a leg of Icelandic lamb and prepare it with all the traditional side dishes, including the previously mentioned sugar-browned potatoes, red cabbage, and green peas. Serving lamb is especially meaningful to me, because the last conversation I had with my father before he unexpectedly passed away on December 27th, 2004, was about how to prepare a leg of lamb, something which he was a master at. In addition to being a good cook, my father was a true food connoisseur. Quite often he showed such appreciation for his food while eating, that even though I was having the same thing he was, I remember looking at his plate wondering if he had something better. That sentiment was echoed by many of his friends at his funeral.

If there is any rigidity surrounding our efforts to preserve language, customs, and food, it surely comes from me and Johanna, because our kids can quite happily adapt and change. There have even been a few instances when my son has explicitly said, "But dad, that's not how we do it here."

Overall, changing traditions has probably been easier for us, simply because we didn't keep that many in the first place. While it is true that traditions bring a certain degree of psychological comfort, we have found that the ability to relax and be flexible instead of "having to do something a certain way" also has many benefits.

When all is said and done, we didn't move away from Iceland to bring every tradition and cultural aspect with us. Instead, our goal is to find a measure of balance between adapting to U.S. culture and preserving our Icelandic heritage.

—Chapter 9—

Deciding to Become a Citizen

He escorted me into his office, where he left me alone for about ten minutes. His walls were covered with accolades and training certificates. Judging from his surroundings, this guy seemed to be really dedicated to his job.

From the time I knew that my wife had been a U.S. citizen from birth, it has been my goal to become a citizen as well. Initially, I wanted to have the same rights as my wife and two children. I realized that I could lose the green card if I stayed outside of the U.S. for longer than one year at a time without getting special permission. I felt that it was important for all four of us to have the same rights. On the other hand, I confess that during the citizenship application process the founding principles of this country have grown on me. I have come to believe in the ideal that "We the

"You Can't Have the Green Card"

People" can come together "to form a more perfect Union". The United States represent the most awesome social experiment in the world — a melting pot of cultures, united behind the idea of living free in a democratic Republic.

At the same time, I am not blind to the difficulties facing this nation, nor am I unaware of the fact that many of the founding principles have either been diluted over the years or not allowed to properly evolve along with society. There are many things to criticize in the USA, and thanks to freedom of speech, everyone is allowed to voice their criticism — something that the 24 hour news media has become particularly good at. However, I don't think that what I have observed in the media represents the everyday reality of living in the USA. My perception is that Americans are hard on America's shortcomings because they believe that the society can get better, and that is a vision I share as well.

*   *   *

While I don't want to venture too far into the discussion of politics, I would be remiss if I did not include a few words about my political heritage. In

Deciding to Become a Citizen

Iceland, we have a multi-party parliamentary system. Because the country is very small, everyone is engaged in politics in one way or another from an early age. Government policies are hotly debated in all kinds of social gatherings — from the family table to the workplace. However, because of the multi-party system, and the fact that different parties have similar policies in one matter while totally opposing each other in another, it is possible to discuss politics without revealing who you are voting for — and, because the government is usually comprised of a multi-party coalition, compromise is central to the political process.

While I was growing up, I remember politics being debated all around me without the debate resulting in permanent rifts between people (this may have been different between gatherings, but the overall sentiment in the country was that one could talk politics without creating enemies).

I learned to see debates and compromise as important aspects of the political process. Debate flushed out a variety of perspectives, and it was not unknown to see people change their minds during these discussions. I always found it fascinating to engage in political dialogues without necessarily revealing who I was voting for. Thusly,

"You Can't Have the Green Card"

I was brought up to believe that the ability to defend one's viewpoint while also exposing oneself to different viewpoints, is the cornerstone needed to sustain democratic principles. My father used to press me for my opinions saying: "Don't say 'just because'. Tell me *why* you believe that?"

I can safely say that my political heritage, which is something that I intend to pass on to my children, is the idea that *dialogue* is central to the democratic process. In an era when people mostly talk politics at each other, rather than talking to each other, I believe that my heritage may be of some value.

Yet, the vile political rhetoric that has been ongoing in the USA for the past few years has made me doubt my reasons for becoming a U.S. citizen a few times — but not enough to change my mind. Despite what the world may think of America, the truth is that more people want to get in than want to get out. On balance, I like living here, and when all is said and done, that is enough.

*   *   *

When I was eligible to become a U.S. citizen, the process didn't take very long. Being married to

Deciding to Become a Citizen

a U.S. citizen, and coming from Iceland, a country that doesn't exactly pose a threat to the USA (or any other country), must have expedited the process quite a bit. As the spouse of a citizen, I was allowed to submit my application for naturalization after living in the USA for *three years*. During my mother's stay with us in the summer of 2013, she gave me the application fee as a pre-birthday present, which allowed me to submit my N-400 application in June that year. In contrast to the green card application, the naturalization form was easy to fill in.

A mere month after I mailed the application, I was summoned in for biometric confirmation, which consisted of fingerprinting and taking pictures. I was then put through an FBI background check — a process that I probably would not have known about if they hadn't told me it was going on. After I had successfully passed the FBI background check, I was given an interview date, also referred to as the Naturalization Test. To prepare for the test, I got a book and a CD with 100 questions and answers about U.S. governance, U.S. geography and U.S. history. In order to pass the test, I was told that I had to answer 6 out of 10 random questions from a list of 100 correctly. Most of the questions were common knowledge and without any preparation I answered 76 out of 100 correctly on my first try. Not wanting to leave anything to chance, I used the month of August to fill in the gaps, and on the day before I left for my interview in San Antonio in September, I answered 100 out of 100 questions correctly when my wife questioned me.

Once I was in San Antonio on September 16, having waited for an hour in the parking lot, I entered the Homeland Security building, a rather stuffy and bland government structure. The agent who greeted me for my interview was of Latino origin, about five feet tall, thin, with a receding hairline, much like mine. He escorted me into his office, where he left me alone for about ten minutes. His walls were covered with accolades and training certificates. Judging from his surroundings, this guy seemed to be really dedicated to his job.

The interview itself only took about twenty minutes. First the agent administered the civics test. I answered the first six questions correctly. At that point he told me that I had passed and that he didn't have to ask me more questions.

Deciding to Become a Citizen

To give you an example of what is required of applicants, I present you with **ten random questions** and acceptable answers from the naturalization test.

Q: What is an amendment?
A change (to the Constitution)
An addition (to the Constitution)

Q: What is freedom of religion?
You can practice any religion,
or not practice a religion

Q: How many U.S. Senators are there?
One hundred (100)

Q: If both the President and the Vice President can no longer serve, who becomes President?
The Speaker of the House

Q: Who wrote the Declaration of Independence?
(*Thomas*) Jefferson

Q: When was the Constitution written?
1787

"You Can't Have the Green Card"

Q: Who was President during the Great Depression and World War II?
(*Franklin*) Roosevelt

Q: What ocean is on the West Coast of the United States?
Pacific (*Ocean*)

Q: Why does the flag have 13 stripes?
Because there were 13 original colonies
Because the stripes represent the original colonies

Q: When is the last day you can send in federal income tax forms?
April 15

When it came to the oral English test, it consisted of reading one of three sentences correctly in order to pass. It was *too easy*. The same was true of the written test. The agent read out a simple sentence and I was supposed to write it correctly. I did and passed. The kicker was that I would have gotten *two more chances* had I failed on my first try.

It really surprised me how low the bar was set on the English exam. As I understand it, the main difference between being a permanent resident

Deciding to Become a Citizen

(having the green card) and being a U.S. citizen is the ability to vote. Decent language skills are imperative if one is to engage in societal reform and civic dialogue—both of which are central components of citizenship. I say this not to imply that people who don't speak English should be denied admittance to the USA (as that would be rather disingenuous after describing our efforts to preserve Icelandic in the previous chapter), but rather to point out that having a green card is more than sufficient for those who want to create a life here without political engagement. Becoming a U.S. citizen carries with it both rights and responsibilities, and based on everything I know, citizenship requires proficient English skills.

*   *   *

Once the agent had administered the civics and language tests, which took about seven minutes combined, the rest of the time was dedicated to double checking all the answers I had given on my N-400 application. Even though I found the process redundant, I answered every single question truthfully. When the interview was over, the agent told me that I had passed with flying colors and that I would be recommended for naturalization.

"You Can't Have the Green Card"

I called my wife immediately, and she was overjoyed to hear the news. "Now you can vote," she said with pride in her voice. To put her initial reaction into perspective, voting turnout is usually high in Iceland, between eighty to ninety percent, sometimes higher. Once there was a referendum election and only sixty percent participated. There was actual talk of annulling the results because of low voter turnout. While I see that many people in the USA are fed up with politics, the irony is that they don't have a voice unless they participate in the process. The best way to influence the outcome is still to *show up and vote*.

* * *

On my two hour drive back to Austin that day, I reflected on what it meant to be a citizen of a country this size — *one thousand times bigger* than the one I was brought up in. I thought about how I could contribute to society in a meaningful way. Thousands of thoughts ran through my mind on the drive back home, all of them revolving around the question: "What does it mean to be a good citizen?" While pondering those thoughts created more questions than answers, something within

Deciding to Become a Citizen

me stirred that day. The thinking process revealed a real need to be more than an observer. I felt the urge to become an active participant and play a constructive role in the society that I had chosen to live in.

—Chapter 10—

The Day I Became a U.S. Citizen

Before we took the oath, the 50 countries represented were called out, and the people from each country asked to stand. I was the only one from Iceland.

Merely four months after I had submitted my N-400 application for U.S. citizenship, I was scheduled to appear before a federal judge in San Antonio to pledge my oath of allegiance to the United States of America, and to receive my certificate of naturalization. The date of the swearing in ceremony was set for October 24, 2013 — four days after my father would have turned seventy five, and one day before my mother turned sixty three.

Early in the month of October there was a partial government shutdown in Washington, and for a period I thought the ceremony might have to be

"You Can't Have the Green Card"

postponed, but a week before I was to be naturalized the stalemate was resolved.

On the day of my naturalization ceremony, I woke up early and made pancakes for the whole family. My wife and I wanted our children to accompany us to the ceremony, and our decision was supported by their teachers. Our "field trip" was even discussed at a later date as part of a civics lesson in their 5th Grade and Kindergarten classes respectively.

It was a beautiful day in San Antonio, sunny, but not too hot. It took just over an hour for the line of prospective citizens to be admitted into the Institute of Texan Cultures and processed once inside. We then waited another two hours for the ceremony to start. Fortunately the institute is a fascinating museum of Texan culture and history. My wife toured it extensively with our kids, who still talk about all the things they saw that day.

The ceremony took place in a large dome shaped area, which had been cordoned off with ropes and transformed into a federal courtroom. There were 237 people from 50 different countries sworn in as U.S. citizens that day.

The American flag was raised at the start of the ceremony, and we enjoyed patriotic music from an army band. The honorable Xavier Rodriguez began the ceremony by talking about his origins in Mexico. He spoke about how he had served in the U.S. military, mentioned that he and his four brothers sported eight University degrees between them, and expressed how he felt that anything was possible—all thanks to the United States of America. It crossed my mind that, without a strong government *of the people* that works *for the people*, none of that would have been possible.

Before we took the oath, the 50 countries represented were called out, and the people from each country were asked to stand. I was the only one from Iceland. The names of the countries were announced in alphabetical order, but to my surprise the announcer omitted Mexico. There was a reason. At the very end, she said: "And last but not least, Mexico." At that point my wife—who was observing the ceremony from outside the ropes—told me that half the room stood up. I sat next to a guy who was originally from Mexico, but had been in the USA since early in his childhood. He was my age, a business owner in Round Rock, an American through and through, but was only getting his citizenship now.

"You Can't Have the Green Card"

When everyone was standing, the judge administered the oath of allegiance. I confess that after I had taken the oath, and the army band played the *Star Spangled Banner*, the overwhelming emotions brought tears to my eyes. It was a bigger moment than I had expected.

After the group took the oath we were shown a video which included part of John F. Kennedy's iconic inaugural address, including the now famous words: "Ask not what your country can do for you, ask what you can do for your country". At the very end of the ceremony all of us were presented with official Certificates of Naturalization and a variety of reading materials, including a copy of the U.S. Constitution. Before leaving, I registered to vote and had my picture taken with the honorable Xavier Rodriguez. I walked out of the Institute of Texan Cultures feeling great — like a valued member of American society.

*   *   *

Later that day, we dined at our favorite BBQ restaurant in Austin called Rudy's. Before I moved to Texas, BBQ meant the same as grilling, but after living here for several years, I understand that when a Texan talks about BBQ, he means smoked brisket, ribs, and sausage.

When we finally arrived at our house in Austin around 6 PM, a place that we had moved into a year earlier, all our neighbors stood outside celebrating my homecoming as a citizen. That was a great surprise. My wife had organized the event and had even bought large letters that the neighbors had put up on our garage door spelling out "Congratulations Gudjon U.S. citizen".

We have truly been blessed with storybook neighbors this past year, people who have gone out of their way to help us in more ways than one. The best examples are Cathy, a retired high school math teacher from across the street, and her husband Fred, a retired minister, who have halfway adopted our children. My kids run and hug Cathy every time they see her, and my son practices piano at their house every single day. We couldn't ask for better neighbors. It pains us to have to leave this place in 2014, but that is one of the downsides of renting.

After I had hugged everyone, I paraded the naturalization certificate around and was surprised to hear that most of my neighbors had not seen one before.

"You Can't Have the Green Card"

Once we said our goodbyes and the kids had settled down, I turned on the TV and watched game two of the World Series in baseball, which featured the Red Sox against the Cardinals. The Cardinals won that game, but the bearded Red Sox deservedly won the series. While I was watching that baseball game, I thought fondly back to our trip to Houston in 2009 when Russ took me and Daniel to an Astros game and taught us the rules. I don't much care who wins or loses during the 162 game regular baseball season, but I really like watching the postseason, when every single pitch counts.

Since we moved to the USA, I have become quite the sports fan. The interest started because of proximity, but in three years, passive observation has grown into significant interest. I was never into sports in Iceland — even prided myself on being the anti-sports guy — so it's been quite a turnaround for Johanna who didn't marry a sports fan. I am by no means a diehard fan, and can usually regain my composure within minutes when a team that I am cheering for suffers a loss — with the exception of the Spurs losing the NBA title to the Heat in 2013. I was invested in that series, and it took a while to get over it. The unexpected upside is that my genuine interest in sports usually gives me something to talk about in social circumstances — especially when talking about religion and politics is out of the question.

*   *   *

After watching the baseball game that night, Johanna and I started reminiscing and talked for over an hour about everything that had happened. It was then that I decided to *write this book*. Recounting all the events that had led to my naturalization seemed more like fiction than fact. Our story deserved to be told.

When I finally went to bed, I first read the complete Declaration of Independence and then started reading the Constitution. The last words I read before going to sleep were:

"We the People of the United States, in Order to form a more perfect Union, establish Justice, insure domestic Tranquility, provide for the common defense, promote the general Welfare, and secure the Blessings of Liberty to ourselves and our Posterity, do ordain and establish this Constitution for the United States of America."

"You Can't Have the Green Card"

I smiled. For better or for worse, I had become a U.S. citizen, a valid member of a Republic that was founded on principles of self-governance by immigrants for immigrants. It is an honor and duty that I intend to take seriously.

—Chapter 11—

Appetite for U.S. History

Historian Will Durant said that since history repeats itself, the news at night should be eighty percent history and twenty percent current events – and even the current events should be explained in the light of history.

As a newly minted U.S. citizen, I feel a sense of belonging and have committed myself to learning as much about civic engagement and U.S. history as I can. Reflecting on what little I have learned about the U.S. Constitution, it seems to have been deliberately set up to force compromise with its checks and balances. I know, for example, that it took more than six hundred separate votes to settle disputes during the creation of the Constitution, which makes the document a primary example of compromise. Learning about historical events, from colonial times to the era of the founding fathers, the civil war and beyond, has opened my eyes in more ways than one. Fortunately, my discoveries have only increased my appetite for history. I especially enjoy learning about the U.S. Presidents and how they have influenced the country's trajectory. I was surprised to learn that George Washington specifically warned against the formation of political parties or factions in one of his farewell addresses. It was as though he could see far into the future and predict the resulting divisions.

* * *

To echo a fraction of what I have learned, I would like to share the following Presidential quotes — some of which are relevant to our current political climate.

On Hope for the Future

"I must study politics and war that my sons may have liberty to study mathematics and philosophy."
—John Adams

On Respectful Dialogue

"I never considered a difference of opinion in politics, in religion, in philosophy, as cause for withdrawing from a friend."
—Thomas Jefferson

On the Importance of Thinking

"Too often we... enjoy the comfort of opinion without the discomfort of thought."
—John F. Kennedy

On Democratic Government

"Of our political revolution of '76, we all are justly proud. It has given us a degree of political freedom, far exceeding that of any other nation of the earth. In it the world has found a solution of the long mooted problem, as to the capability of man to govern himself. In it was the germ which has vegetated, and still is to grow and expand into the universal liberty of mankind."
—Abraham Lincoln

"You Can't Have the Green Card"

On the Importance of Immigration

"The land flourished because it was fed from so many sources — because it was nourished by so many cultures and traditions and peoples."
—Lyndon B. Johnson

On the Importance of Voting

"Nobody will ever deprive the American people of the right to vote except the American people themselves and the only way they could do this is by not voting."
—Franklin D. Roosevelt

Knowing history is important. Historian Will Durant said that since history repeats itself, the news at night should be eighty percent history and twenty percent current events — and even the current events should be explained in the light of history. While I doubt that news networks will change their approach and start reporting based on these parameters, I know that my appetite for history has increased and that I will undoubtedly continue to discover more — both about the uplifting parts of U.S. history and the darker aspects.

Appetite for U.S. History

History is a great teacher, and I am a willing student.

—Chapter 12—

Enjoying the Mystery

As I look to the future, the adventurer in me is looking forward to seeing how my life in the USA turns out. I will continue to act on my intuition and put myself out there, not knowing how the moving parts in the universe will respond.

As I revisit my story and examine all the twists and turns, most of which I could never have orchestrated through my own efforts, I must reiterate my initial belief, which is that I could not *not* be here. Yes, I could have reacted differently to some of what has transpired, but the number of synchronous events that got me to the States verges on the ridiculous. The world certainly does work in mysterious ways. While some people think they have gotten a handle on these synchronicities, calling them spiritual principles of manifesting, I must side with the late Jim Rohn, who often

"You Can't Have the Green Card"

proclaimed that he didn't try to understand the mysteries of life, he simply enjoyed them.

In the spirit of mystery I'll leave you with a story that certainly falls into that category — the tale of how I met poet and Rumi translator Coleman Barks in late 2013.

*   *   *

In the late nineties, while I was going through my first yoga teacher training, I was introduced to the spiritual poetry of 12th Century Sufi poet Rumi. I soon bought a compilation of his poems called *The Essential Rumi*, a book that was translated by Coleman Barks. In the years that followed I drew continuous inspiration from Rumi's profound poetry, and in 2005, I was moved to compose music to selected poems by Rumi — music which I then recorded demos of in 2006.

However, I didn't know how intellectual property law affected the translations. I knew that Rumi's works were in the public domain, but I also knew that the same was probably not true about the works of his translator, Coleman Barks. I made several attempts to contact Mr. Barks, but had no luck, so I gave up. I stashed my demos and didn't touch them for several years.

Enjoying the Mystery

Then, in the fall of 2013, I was driving home from a local bookstore when the idea hit me. I should try to contact Coleman Barks again. I ran to the computer as soon as I got home, found his website, and filled out the contact form. Although I did this with some reservations based on my previous unsuccessful attempts, I still did it.

To my surprise, mere fifteen minutes later, I had not only received an answer, but Coleman Barks had personally replied and given me permission to use his translations along with my music.

I was euphoric!

I shared this news at a Men's Fellowship meeting at Unity Church of the Hills, and in a rare appearance at the meeting, the Reverend Stephen Bolen heard my story. Within a couple of days, he sent me an email asking me if he could invite me to a dinner and an evening of Rumi poetry with Coleman Barks at the Interfaith Institute in Austin. Getting to meet Coleman Barks was a dream come true, so I was quick to reply with a resounding yes—feeling and expressing a deep sense of gratitude and anticipation.

The dinner was set for a Sunday evening, a mere two and a half weeks after my correspondence with Mr. Barks. I arrived early that night with

"You Can't Have the Green Card"

my *Essential Rumi* book in hand. The first person I ran into, sitting in a lounge chair in the corridor, was none other than Coleman Barks himself. I approached him, we had a short but interesting conversation, and he signed my book. I then enjoyed a magnificent evening of poetry and history, along with the generous people from UCOH, including Reverend Stephen and his wife Mary. Never in my wildest dreams could I have orchestrated this order of events, but they happened nonetheless, and I enjoyed reveling in the mystery.

*   *   *

As I look to the future, the adventurer in me is looking forward to seeing how my life in the USA turns out. I will continue to act on my intuition and put myself out there, not knowing how the moving parts in the universe will respond.

Thank you for reading my story.

Sincerely,

Gudjon Bergmann

Contact Information

Please feel free to contact Gudjon Bergmann if you have any questions or comments. He will do his best to reply to all emails and looks forward to learning about how his story has affected you. He would also be happy to speak to your group or discuss any of the topics that he mentions in his book.

His email is *gbergmann@gbergmann.com*

His website is *www.gbergmann.com*

Pictures

Gudjon Bergmann (right) with his children Hanna and Daniel and the honorable Judge Xavier Rodriguez (center) on October 24th, 2013.

Gudjon Bergmann outside his garage on the day that he became a U.S. citizen.

Gudjon Bergmann in 2011 with his Mercury Grand Marquis.

Gudjon, Johanna, Hanna, and Daniel on July 4th, 2010, two days after they moved to the USA.

Made in the USA
Charleston, SC
06 March 2014